HISTORICAL MYSTERIES

The Truth Behind the World's Most Perplexing Events and Conspiracies Revealed – Mind-Blowing Stories of Four History's Mysteries and Conspiracy Theories!

BERNADINE CHRISTNER

TABLE OF CONTENTS

THE ESCOVEDO MURDER

'Many a man may trace his downfall to a murder, of which, perhaps, he thought little enough at the time,' writes De Quincey. This comment refers especially to Philip II. of Spain, his secretary, Antonio Perez, Perez's steward, his page, and several professional ruffians. From the King to his scullion, everyone was involved in the assassination of Juan de Escovedo, the secretary of Philip's famed natural brother, Don John of Austria. All of them, to varying degrees, had deep reasons to regret an action that seemed to be a routine political occurrence at the time.

The mystery in the case of Escovedo is neither the method in which he disappeared nor the identities of his killers. These facts are widely known; the identities of those responsible, from the King to the bravo, are known. However, obscurity obscures the motivations for the action. Why was Escovedo executed? Did the King slay him for merely political motives, which were insufficient in the first place but were inflated by the suspicious royal fancy? Or were Philip II's secretary and Spain's monarch competitors for the love of a high-ranking one-eyed widow? And did the secretary, Perez, persuade Philip to order Escovedo's killing because Escovedo threatened to divulge their wicked plot to the King? With varying degrees of agreement, Sir William Stirling-Maxwell and Monsieur Mignet accepted this interpretation. Mr. Froude, on the other hand, believed Philip acted for political motives and with the full consent of his ill-informed conscience.

According to Mr. Froude, there was no woman as a motivation in the case. A third possibility is that Philip wanted to kill Escovedo for political reasons, without regard for the sensitive affection. Still, Philip was hesitant and indecisive, while Perez, who feared Escovedo's involvement with his love affair, spurred his royal master on to the crime he was avoiding. We may never know the whole truth, but we may study a condition of morality and manners in Madrid that makes the blundering tragedies of Holyrood in Queen Mary's time seem like child's play. When put against Philip II's instruments, Bothwell's 'lambs' are lively and compassionate.

Escovedo, the slain man, and Antonio Perez, Shakespeare's "first killer," had both been schooled in the service of Ruy Gomez, Philip's famed minister. Gomez had a wife, Aa de Mendoza, who, having been born in 1546, was thirty-two, not thirty-eight (as M. Mignet claims) when Escovedo was assassinated in 1578. However, 1546 might be a typo for 1540. She was blind in one eye in 1578, but both of her eyes were undoubtedly bright in 1567 when she seems to have been Philip's mistress or was widely assumed to be. Eleven years later, at the time of the murder, there is no reason to believe Philip was still susceptible to her charms. Her husband, Prince d'Eboli, had died in 1573 (or, as Mr. Froude says, in 1567); the Princess was now a widow, and if she chose to distinguish her husband's old secretary, at this date the King's secretary, Antonio Perez, there seems no reason to suppose that Philip would have been bothered by the matter. M. Mignet's view of the sufficient cause of Escovedo's murder is that he still loved Aa with an unroyal fidelity, that she loved Perez, and that she and Perez feared Escovedo would betray them to the King. Mignet, on the other hand, believes, and correctly so, that Philip had made up his mind, as far as he ever did, to assassinate Escovedo long before that diplomatist became an uncomfortable spy on the alleged lovers.

To get things up to the tragic level of Euripides' Phdra, Perez was believed to be the natural son of his late boss, Gomez, the spouse of his supposed lover. Perez was most likely nothing of the such; he was the bastard of a man of his name. His supposed mistress, Gomez's widow, may have even disseminated the other tale to establish that her ties with Perez, albeit personal, were innocent. They are a lovely group of folks!

Escovedo and Perez have been buddies since they were children. While Perez moved from Gomez's service to Philip's, Escovedo was appointed secretary to the nobly daring Don John of Austria in 1572. The Court thought he was supposed to be a spy on Don John, but he succumbed to the charms of that brave heart and gladly accepted, if not inspired, the most audacious designs of the winner of Lepanto, the Sword of Christendom. This was highly uncomfortable for the leaden-footed Philip, who never took time by the forelock, but instead brooded on projects and passed up opportunities. Don John, on the other hand, was all for pressing the game. When he was dispatched to tempt and conciliate in the Low Countries and remove the Spanish army of occupation, he planned to transfer the Spanish men out of the Netherlands via water. He would descend on England once they were on the blue sea, rescue the prisoner Mary Stuart, marry her (he was fearless!), reestablish the Catholic faith, and assume the English crown. A solid plan, authorized by the Pope, but one that did not fit Philip's mind. He set his leaden foot on the concept and several other brave undertakings designed in the finest Alexandre Dumas tradition. Now, to whom Don John was devotedly attached, Escovedo was the essence of all these chivalrous schemes, and Philip saw him as a very dangerous person as a result.

When Don John first visited the Low Countries, Escovedo was in Madrid (1576). He persisted in pressing Philip to adopt Don John's ardent suggestions, despite Antonio Perez's requests to be careful. Perez was Escovedo's buddy on this day, 1576. But Escovedo was not to be counseled; instead, he sent an agitated letter to the King, criticizing his stitchless policy (descosido), dilatory, shambling, and idealess operations. According to Sir William Stirling-Don Maxwell's John of Austria, "the term employed by Escovedo was descosido, unstitched." However, Mr. Froude claims that Philip subsequently repeated the phrase regarding another letter from Escovedo, which he also referred to as a "bloody letter" (January 1578). Mr. Froude is unlikely to be correct here since Philip's letter containing that filthy term was written in July 1577.

In any event, Philip was persuaded to ignore the error in

1576 by Perez's pleading, and Escovedo, whose presence Don John sought, was sent to him in December 1576. Don John and Escovedo began writing to their friend Perez on this day, and Perez enticed them by showing their letters to the King. Just as Charles I. commissioned the Duke of Hamilton to spy on the Covenanted nobility, pretending to sympathize with them and speaking in their holy manner, Philip gave Perez instructions to capture Don John and Escovedo. 'I want no theology but my own to defend myself,' Perez remarked, and Philip responded, 'My theology takes the same view of the problem as yours.'

According to M. Mignet's hypothesis, at this time, 1577, Perez, although a gambler and a profligate who accepted gifts from all hands, must have intended nothing worse than serving Philip as he liked to be served to keep him fully informed of Don John's ambitions. According to M. Mignet, Escovedo was not yet an impediment to Perez's and the King's mistress, Princess Eboli's amours. On the other hand, Sir William Stirling-Maxwell believes that Perez's goal was to destroy Don John; Sir William admits that he does not know why. On the other hand, Perez had no such goal until Don John confided in him initiatives that were subversive or hazardous to the Government of his lord, the King.

Did Don John, or Escovedo, entrust Perez with plans that were not only chivalrous and impractical but also traitorous? Don John, on the other hand, did nothing of the like. Escovedo abandoned him and traveled to Spain without being summoned, arriving in July 1577. Don John beat the Dutch

Protestants at the battle of Gemblours on January 31, 1578, while he was away. He then addressed a letter to Escovedo and Perez in Madrid, full of chivalrous devotion. He would make Philip the true lord of the Low Countries, and he urged Escovedo and Perez to instill resolve in the King. That was unthinkable because Philip could never have wanted to assassinate Escovedo just because he had pleaded for assistance for Don John. Yet, as soon as Escovedo announced his return to Spain in July 1577, Philip remarked in a letter to Perez, 'we must dispatch him before he kills us.' There seems to be no question that the letter in which this sentence appears is real, even though we only have a copy of it. The sentence, however, appropriately translated? 'priest á despacherle antes que nos mate' (Escovedo) translates as 'we must be swift and dispatch him before he kills us.' Mr. Froude, who is far kinder to Philip than to Mary Stuart, recommends translating the line "we must dispatch Escovedo promptly" (i.e., send him on his way) as "before he scares us to death." Mr. Froude so disputes that Philip intended to assassinate Escovedo in 1577. If the King uttered the words twice, it is bad for Mr. Froude's argument and Philip's reputation. In March 1578, he wrote to Perez about Escovedo, telling him to 'act fast before nos mate—before he murders us.' At least, that's what Perez said, but is his date correct? Perez did act this time, and Escovedo was slaughtered! If Perez is correct, Philip meant what he stated in 1577 when he declared, 'Despatch him before he murders us.'

Why did Philip fear Escovedo so much? We only have

Perez's public words in his description of the incident. Perez adds a unique allegation against Escovedo after explaining the basic reasons for Philip's fear of Don John and the notions that a very skeptical monarch would have entertained, given his brother's adventurous nature. According to Perez, he pledged that after conquering England, he and Don John would invade Spain. Escovedo requested the captaincy of a castle perched on a cliff overlooking Santander's harbor; he was the town's alcalde. He and Don John intended to utilize this citadel against their ruler so that Aramis and Fouquet intended to exploit Belle Isle in Dumas' book. In truth, Escovedo had requested the leadership of Mogro, the castle controlling Santander, in the spring of 1577, and Perez notified Philip that the site should be improved for the safety of the harbor, but not given to Escovedo. Don John's allegiance could never have imagined the use of the location as a stronghold to be held in the event of an assault on his King. But, if Perez held no resentment against Escovedo in 1577 as being harmful to his purported amour with the Princess Eboli, then Philip's deadly plot must have sprung from the deep suspiciousness of his temperament, not from Perez's promptings.

Escovedo arrived in Spain in July 1577. He was not slain until March 31, 1578, despite many attempts on his life a few weeks before. M. Mignet contends that Philip held his hand until the early spring of 1578 because Perez calmed his fears; that Escovedo then threatened to reveal Perez's love affair to his royal rival; and that Perez, in his private interest, now changed his tune and, instead of appeasing Philip, urged him to commit the crime. But Philip was so sluggish that he couldn't even perform a murder with reasonable haste. Even in his view, Escovedo was not dangerous while he was apart from Don John. But as the weeks passed, Don John maintained demanding Escovedo's return by letter. For that reason, maybe, Philip pushed his bravery to the (literally)'sticking' point, and Escovedo became stuck.' On the other hand, Major Martin Hume claims that conditions had changed, and Philip had no reason to kill.

M. Mignet and Sir William Stirling-Maxwell, Don John's biographer, have quite different perspectives. They claim that in 1578, Princess Eboli was Philip's lover; she duped him with Perez, that Escovedo threatened to reveal everything, and that Perez then murdered Philip. Would Escovedo have consistently accepted Perez's dinner invites if this had been the case? If Escovedo were threatening Perez, the men would have been on the worst of terms, yet Escovedo continued to dine with Perez. Again, Perez's approach would have been to send Escovedo where he wanted to go, to Flanders, far away from Don John. It is likely, but not proven, that the Princess and Philip were lovers around 1567. However, it isn't very certain, and not proven, that Philip was still dedicated to the woman in 1578. The Mendozas, some of the Princess's relatives, now intended to assassinate Perez as a disgrace to their heritage. Later, during Perez's trial, substantial evidence proved that he loved the Princess or was suspected of doing so, but it is not established that this was an issue that Philip was concerned about. Thus, it is not impossible that Escovedo despised Perez and the Princess's relationship, but nothing suggests that he might have put himself at risk by disclosing them to the King. Furthermore, if he had spoken his thoughts to Perez about the affair, the two would not have continued on terms of the most amicable contact, as they seemed to have done. A Perez squire recalled a scenario in which Escovedo threatened to condemn the Princess, but how did the squire become a witness to the episode in which the Princess challenged Escovedo with great coarseness?

In any case, when Philip contacted the Marquis of Los Velez about the appropriateness of executing Escovedo rather than returning him to Don John, the Marquis was persuaded by ordinary political suspicions.

It was a matter of conscience at the time as to whether a king might have a subject slain if the royal motivations, though substantial, could not be exposed safely in a court of law. On these grounds, Queen Mary had the authority to detain Darnley for good political reasons that could not be made public; for international reasons. On the other hand, Mary did not consult her confessor, who felt she was innocent of her husband's murder. Philip's confessor informed him that the King had complete authority to dispatch Escovedo, and Philip delivered his instructions to Perez. According to Perez, he reiterated his comments from 1577 in 1578: 'Make haste before he murders us.'

In this matter of conscience, the authority of a king to inflict murder on a subject for political purposes, Protestant thinking seems to have been forgiving. When the Ruthvens were assassinated on August 5, 1600, at Perth, in the most enigmatic of all mysteries, the Rev. Robert Bruce, a staunch Presbyterian, refused to accept that James VI. had not plotted their death. 'But your Majesty could have hidden motives,' Bruce remarked to the King, who, of course, maintained his innocence. This seems to indicate that Mr. Bruce, like Philip's confessor, believed that a monarch had the authority to kill a subject for hidden State purposes. The concept was fiercely condemned by the Inquisition when a Spanish preacher held it, yet Knox approved King Henry's (Darnley's) murder of Riccio. On this issue, I sympathize with the Inquisition.

Perez, who had been tasked with organizing the crime, delegated the task to

Martinez serves as his steward. Martinez asked a rough-looking page, Enriquez, whether he knew "someone in my nation" (Murcia) "who would thrust a knife into a person." 'I shall talk about it to a muleteer of my acquaintance,' Enriquez replied, 'which I did, and the muleteer undertook the job.' However, when Enriquez learned that a man of significance was about to be knifed, he warned Perez that a muleteer was not noble enough and that the job must be given to individuals of greater respect.'

Enriquez confessed in 1585 for a legitimate reason: Perez had grossly mishandled the firm. All kinds of individuals were engaged, and after the murder, they fled and started to die in an alarmingly regular fashion. Naturally, Enriquez assumed

Perez was behaving similarly to Mures of Auchendrane, who sent a slew of witnesses and collaborators in their assassination of Kennedy. Because they constantly required a new accomplice to murder the previous accomplice, then another to slaughter the slayer, and so on, the Mures would have depopulated Scotland if left uncontrolled. Enriquez predicted that his time to die would come soon, so he confessed, which Diego Martinez confirmed. As a result, the truth was revealed, and murderers should take note.

Perez was resolved to poison Escovedo while the muleteer hung fire. But he had no idea how to go about doing it. Science was still in its infancy for her. To poison a guy in Scotland, you had to depend on a vulgar witch or send a guy to France, at a considerable price, to get the poison, and the messenger was discovered and tortured. The Spanish Court was not more scientific.

Martinez sent Enriquez to Murcia to collect toxic plants, which a venal pharmacist distilled. The toxin was subsequently tested on a barnyard bird, which did not fare any better. On the other hand, Martinez managed to get specific water that was good to be offered as a drink.' Perez invited Escovedo to dinner, Enriquez sat at the table, and in each cup of wine Escovedo drank, he added 'a nutshell of the water,' quite homeopathically. Escovedo was no more poisoned than the previous experiment's cock. 'It was determined that the beverage had no impact at all.'

Escovedo dined with the kind Perez again a few days later.

They offered him some white powder in a dish of cream on this occasion, as well as the poisoned water in his wine, considering it a shame to squander that beverage. Unfortunately, this time Escovedo was ill, and Enriquez tricked a scullion in the royal kitchen into putting more of the powder in a bowl of soup at Escovedo's dwelling. For this, the unfortunate kitchenmaid who made the soup was hung in Madrid's public Plaza, without apologies.

Is Philip was destroying the morale of his people at an alarming pace! However, it is impossible to cook an omelet without breaking eggs. Philip slaughtered the girl in his kitchen as if he had grabbed a rifle and shot her, yet the royal confessor undoubtedly declared that everything was OK.

Despite the resources of Spanish science, Escovedo continued to live, and Perez judged that he had to be shot or stabbed. So Enriquez traveled to his home country in search of an assassin and "a stiletto with a very fine blade, far better than a handgun to murder a guy with." Enriquez, to retain a good thing in the family, enrolled his brother; and Martinez, from Aragon, brought 'two suitable types of men,' Juan de Nera and Insausti, who undertook the duty with the King's scullion. Perez traveled to Alcala for Holy Week, much as the excellent Regent Murray left Edinburgh after preaching on the morning of Darnley's murder. Both gentlemen's motto was 'Have an alibi.'

On the evening of Easter Monday, the underlings pursued Escovedo. Enriquez did not come across him, but Insausti completed his task with a single push in a skillful manner. The scullion rushed to Alcala and informed Perez, who was 'overjoyed.'

We part ways with this noble and devoted servant and move our attention to Don John. When he heard the news from afar, he had no illusions about love relationships being the root of the crime. 'In sadness greater than I can explain,' he wrote to his unhappy brother, the King. He said that the King had lost his finest servant, a "guy without the objectives and skill that are currently in fashion." 'I may have just considered myself to be the cause of his death,' the blow was aimed squarely at Don John. He showed heartfelt concern for Escovedo's wife and children, who died impoverished because (unlike Perez) 'he had clean hands.' By the love of our Lord, he begged Philip to "exercise all conceivable care to ascertain where the blow originated from and to punish it with the harshness which it merits." He will personally settle the dead's most urgent bills. (Beaumont, 20 April 1578.)

This letter most likely astounded the royal caitiff. On September 20, Don John addressed his last letter to his brother, expressing his need for a decision from your Majesty. 'Give me instruction on how to run matters!' 'I will not respond,' Philip scribbled in the margin. Don John, on the other hand, had concluded his letter. 'Our lives are on the line, and all we ask is that we die with honor.' These are the last lines of the famous Montrose's farewell letter to Charles II: "with the greater alacrity and ardor I go to find my death."

Don John, like Montrose, 'took loyalty and honor to the grave.' He died on October 1st, following a long illness. According to Brantôme, he was poisoned by the King on the orders of Perez, and the side of his breast was yellow and black as if scorched and disintegrated at the touch. When a great person died in his bed, these words were invariably said. They are most likely false, but a king who can kill his brother's friend conscientiously may also kill his brother conscientiously and for the same reasons.

Princess Eboli compensated and protected one of Escovedo's killers. They were all rewarded with gold chains, silver cups, an abundance of golden écus, and army appointments; all were transported out of the nation, and some started to die mysteriously, which, as we saw, scared Enriquez into confessing (1585).

Perez was immediately suspected. He made a sympathy call to young Escovedo: he talked about Escovedo's love affair in Flanders; an aggrieved spouse must be the guilty guy! However, skepticism grew. Perez protested to the King about being pursued, scrutinized, and cross-examined by the alcalde and his son. Vasquez, another royal secretary, was a friend of the Escovedo family. Knowing nothing of the King's guilt, and envious of Perez, he continued telling the King that Perez was guilty: that there was a courtship, discovered by Escovedo: that Escovedo died for the love of a woman: that Philip must examine the matter and put an end to the scandal. The lady in question was, of course, Princess Eboli. Philip didn't care about her anymore, at least not just now. According to Mr. Froude, Don Gaspar Moro's investigation on the Princess "has thoroughly refuted the alleged relationship between the Princess and Philip II."

On the other hand, Philip was deeply involved in property litigations against the Princess, which Vasquez handled, while Perez naturally sided with his benefactor's widow. Vasquez's letters on these topics number in the hundreds. Meanwhile, he went, and the Escovedo family fled, leaving no stone unturned in their pursuit of proof that Perez killed Escovedo because Escovedo foiled his courtship with the Princess.

Philip has often vowed to support Perez. But the affair was coming to light, and if it had to come out, Philip preferred that Vasquez pursue Perez on the wrong scent, the fragrance of the courtship, rather than the correct smell, which went directly to the throne and the wretch who sat on it. Neither approach, however, could be very appealing to the King.

Perez accepted to face trial even though no proof could be uncovered against him. His co-conspirators were far away; he would be forgiven, just as Bothwell had been cleared of Darnley's killing. Philip was unable to face the issue. He ordered Perez to consult the President of the Council, De Pazos, a Bishop, and tell him everything while De Pazos consoled little Escovedo. The Bishop, a casuist, told young Escovedo that Perez and the Princess were "as innocent as me." The Bishop disagreed with the Inquisition, claiming that Perez was innocent because he only carried out the King's murderous orders. Young Escovedo fled, but Vasquez persisted, and in a letter to the King, Princess Eboli referred to Vasquez as a "Morish hound." Philip arrested both Perez and the Princess since Vasquez was not to be set down; his job connected with the litigations was to chase the Princess, and Philip couldn't inform Vasquez that he was on the wrong path. The lady was returned to her lands, which gratified Vasquez, and Perez and he were bound to maintain the peace. But suspicion hovered about Perez, and Philip wanted that it did. The secretary was charged with peculation, having accepted bribes on all hands, and he was condemned to huge penalties and jail (January 1585). Now that Enriquez had confessed, a type of covert investigation, the records of which still exist, dragged its plodding course. Perez was being held in residence near a church. He jumped out a window and raced inside the church, where civil force ripped open the gates, violated sanctity, and discovered our buddy cowering in the wooden work beneath the roof, all hung with festoons of cobwebs. The Church condemned the judges, but they had captured Perez, and Philip refused to submit to the religious tribunals. Perez, a prisoner, attempted to escape with the help of one of Escovedo's killers, who remained steadfast but failed, while his wife was ill-treated to force him to hand up all of the King's incriminating letters. He did, however, turn over two locked trunks full of paperwork. But his buddy and steward, Martinez, is alleged to have chosen and hidden the royal notes that proved Philip's guilt.

The King assumed he was secure now and didn't bother

checking to see whether his incriminating letters were still in the sealed trunks! At the very least, if he did know they were missing and that Perez could give evidence of his guilt, it is difficult to understand why, with numerous uncertainties and hesitations, he let the covert murder procedure against Perez continue, after a lengthy pause, until 1590. Vasquez cross-examined Perez many times, but there was still just one witness against him: the scoundrel Enriquez. One was insufficient.

A new step has been made. The royal confessor informed Perez that if he disclosed the complete truth and acknowledged publicly that he had acted on royal instructions, he would be safe! When Perez disobeyed, Philip issued another instruction (Jan. 4, 1590). Perez must now divulge the King's motivation for ordering the assassination. If Philip were preparing a trap for Perez, it would only catch him if he couldn't produce the King's incriminating letters, which he still had. Mr. Froude claims that Philip learned via his confessor, and he learned through Perez's wife that the letters were still hidden and could be retrieved. If that were the case, Perez would be secure, but the King's reputation would be ruined.

What were Philip's goals and motivation? Is he going to declare the letters to be forgeries? No other person (at the time) wrote with such a different hand as his; it was the worst in the world. He must have had a loophole; else, he would not have pressured Perez to testify about his crime. He had a loophole, and Perez was aware of it, since otherwise he would have following instructions, recounted the complete tale, and been let free. He didn't do it. Mr. Froude believes he did not believe the royal power would be sufficient to satisfy the judges. But they couldn't convict Perez, a mere accomplice to Philip, without also condemning the King, which the judges couldn't do. Perez, I believe, would have preferred to take his chances with the judges' harshness against their King rather than reject the King's demand to confess everything and therefore suffer torture. He did face the torture, which suggests that he knew Philip might, in some way, avoid the terrible evidence of his letters. According to Major Martin Hume, Philip's loophole was that if Perez disclosed the King's motives for ordering the murder, they would look outmoded at the crime time. Pedro would be solely responsible. In any case, he was tortured.

Like most individuals in his situation, he underestimated his capacity to withstand pain. He lacked the stamina of the younger Auchendrane assassin, Mitchell, or the courageous Jacobite Nevile Payne, tortured almost to death by the servants of the Dutch tyrant, William of Orange. All of them endured the agony and kept their secrets hidden. But 'eight rounds of the rope' opened Perez's lips, whose obstinacy had only caused him considerable difficulty. However, he did not submit Philip's letters as evidence; instead, he claimed that they had been seized from him. However, the following day, Diego Martinez, who had previously denied everything, realized that the game was over and accepted the reality of all that Enriquez had confessed in 1585.

Perez fled about a month after the abuse. His wife was permitted to see him in jail. She had been the strongest, bravest, and most dedicated of women. If she had any cause to be envious of the Princess, which was far from clear, she had forgiven everyone. She had gone to the ends of the world to rescue her spouse. She had flung herself on the confessor of the King in the Dominican church during high mass, insisting that the priest refuse to absolve the King until he released Perez.

Admitted to her husband's jail, she performed the trick that rescued Lord Ogilvy from the Covenanters' cell, as well as Argyle, Nithsdale, and James M. Macgregor. Perez stepped out of jail wearing his wife's gown. We might assume that the guards were bribed: cooperation is always present in these situations. One of the killers had horses around the corner, and Perez, who the rack could not have seriously hurt, rode thirty miles and passed the Aragon border.

We are not required to follow his subsequent exploits. The reluctance of the Aragonese to surrender him to Castile and their rescue of him from the Inquisition lost them their constitution, and around seventy of them were burnt as heretics. But Perez was able to get away. He visited France, where Henry IV befriended him, and England, where Bacon hosted him. He published his Relaciones in 1594 (?) and informed the world of the tale of Philip's conscience. Of course, that narrative cannot be trusted, and Philip's signed letters regarding Escovedo's murder have been lost. However, the copies in the Hague are considered legitimate, and the exciting parts are marked in red ink.

If, after all, Philip had obtained the whole autograph correspondence and Perez had only succeeded in retaining the copies currently in the Hague, we can see why Perez did not confess the King's crime: he had only copies of his proofs to exhibit, and copies were worthless as evidence. On the other hand, however, Perez had the letters.

'Bloody Perez,' as Bacon's mother referred to him, died in Paris in November 1611, outliving the terrible lord he had so diligently served. Queen Elizabeth persuaded Amyas Paulet to assassinate Mary Stuart. Being a man of honor, Paulet declined; he also feared Elizabeth would leave him to the Scots' fury. Perez should have known Philip would forsake him: his stupidity was rewarded with jail, torture, and confiscation, which were hardly more than the man deserved for betraying and murdering Don John of Austria's servant.

Note.—When I wrote this article, I was unaware that Major Martin Hume had addressed the issue in Transactions of the Royal Historical Society, 1894, pp. 71-107, and in Espaoles é Ingleses, 1894, pp. 71-107. (1903). The last piece very certainly reflects Major Hume's last thoughts. He discovered several of Perez's contemporaneous letters among the Additional MSS. of the British Museum (28,269), which augment the copies of other letters burnt after Perez's death in the Hague. Based on these MSS. and other sources unknown to Mr. Froude and Monsieur Mignet (see the second edition of his Antonio Perez; Paris, 1846), major Hume's thesis This took place in late October or early November 1577. The instruction was not then carried out; the reason for the delay is unclear to me. The months passed, and Escovedo's death ceased to be politically desired under changed circumstances, but he became a major annoyance to Perez and his lover, Princess Eboli. Philip never rescinded the murder, but Perez, according to Major Hume, wrongly claims that the King was still intent on carrying it out and that another leader was contacted and approved of it soon before the actual crime. This impression is created by Perez's deft manipulation of dates in his tale. When he killed Escovedo, he was battling for his hand; but Philip, who had never countermanded the crime, remained unconcerned until 1582 when he was in Portugal with Alva. The King now knew that Perez had acted abominably, that he had poisoned his mind against his brother Don Juan, that he had disclosed State secrets to the Princess Eboli, and that he had murdered Escovedo, not in accordance to the royal decree, but as a cover for his revenge. As a result, Philip was harsh with Perez, and his last demand was for Perez to reveal the royal motivations for the destruction of Escovedo. They would be discovered to be out of date when the crime was committed, and Perez would be held accountable.

If I understand Major Hume properly, this is his hypothesis. The theory maintains Philip's moral character as dark as ever: he ordered an assassination that he never even attempted to reverse. His confessor may cheer him, but he understood that the physicians of the Inquisition, like the general opinion of people, rejected the premise that rulers had the authority to condemn and kill, by the blade, those who had not been placed on trial in public.

MYSTERY OF THE KIRKS

No historical issue has perplexed Englishmen more than the nature of the variations between Scotland's numerous Kirks. The Southron discovered that worshipping in a church of the Established Kirk ('The Auld Kirk,') the Free Church, or the United Presbyterian Church (the U.P.'s) was the same thing. The essence of the service was the same. However, the assembly stood at prayers and sat when it sang; and stood when it sang and knelt at prayer at times. There was no specified liturgy in any of the Kirks. I've gone to a Free Kirk that didn't have a pulpit; the pastor stood on an elevated platform, like a speaker in a lecture hall, but such practice is unnecessary. If I'm not mistaken, the Kirks have several collections of hymns, which were formerly regarded as 'things of human fabrication,' and so 'idolatrous.' However, hymns, as well as organs, harmoniums, and other musical instruments, are now in use. As a result, the Kirks' faces are similar and sisterly:

There is no such thing as an all-encompassing face. There are no exceptions, no matter how many decent esse fora.

What is the difference between the Free Church, the Established Church, and the United Presbyterian Church, the Southron used to wonder? If the Southron posed the question to a Scottish acquaintance, the Scottish friend was unlikely to respond. He may be a member of Scotland's 'Episcopal' community, but he's just as uneducated as any Anglican. Or he may not have done these significant studies in Scottish history, which shed light on this enigmatic topic.

Indeed, the whole nature of the enigma has recently transformed, much like the colors in a kaleidoscope. The most prominent colors are no longer 'Auld Kirk,' 'Free Kirk,' and 'U.P.'s,' but 'Auld Kirk,' 'Free Kirk,' and 'United Free Kirk.' The United Free Kirk was formed in 1900 from the ancient 'United Presbyterians' (as old as 1847), with an overwhelming majority of the old Free Kirk, while the Free Kirk of today is made up of a minuscule minority of the old Free Kirk. The latter refused to join the recent merger. The Free Kirk, colloquially known as 'The Wee Frees,' now has the riches that the old Free Kirk's before, in 1900, combined with the United Presbyterians. Thanks to a verdict, it formed the United Free Church (one may easily call it a 'judgment') of the House of Lords (August 1, 1904). It is anticipated that common sense would find an 'out gait,' or issue, from this unpleasant situation. 'Those who are at all receptive to a sense of national dishonor look forward gladly to such a prospect; they have been spectators already too long to the struggle that has separated our tiny corner of Christendom,' said Mr. R.L. Stevenson, then a sage of twenty-four, in 1874. According to R.L.S., the perennial schisms of the Kirk show "something pathetic for the sorrowful man, but painfully amusing for others."

The irony of the current situation is palpable. About half of the Kirk of Scotland ministers deserted their mansions and nice glebes two generations ago for the sake of certain principles. Unfortunately, they abandoned some of these notions or left them in suspense a few years ago, and as a consequence, they have lost, if only for the time being, their manses, stipends, colleges, and attractive glebes.

Why should all of this be the case? The explanation can only be found in the history of the Scottish Reformation, which is both sorrowful and painfully hilarious. When John Knox died on November 24, 1572, a good burgess of Edinburgh wrote in his Diary, 'John Knox, minister, dying, who had, as was said, the most of the blame of all the sufferings of Scotland, since the massacre of the late Cardinal,' Beaton, assassinated at St. Andrews in 1546. Three hundred thirty-two years have passed since his death, and the current woes of the United Free Kirk are direct if the distant outcome of some of John Knox's beliefs.

The whole problem stems from his unusual ideas regarding the relationship between Church and State and his followers. In 1843, half of the ministers of the Established Kirk in Scotland, if not more, left the Kirk and headed into the wilderness in search of what they saw as Knox's ideal. They face a similar exodus in 1904 because they are no longer steadfast supporters of the same goal! Nevertheless, a small minority of around twenty-seven pastors sticks to the Knoxian ideal. All the money lavished to the Free Kirk by devout patrons over the last sixty years is rewarded by all the money lavished to the Free Kirk.

For 344 years (1560-1904), the fight has been about Church-State ties, as we know. According to Lord Macnaghten, who offered one of the two views in favor of the United Free Kirk's claim to the property held by the Free Kirk before its merger with the United Presbyterians in 1900, the rupture of 1843 developed as a result of the Free Kirk's withdrawal from the Established Kirk. According to the sympathetic judge, there were two groups in the Established Church before 1843: the 'Moderates' and the 'Evangelicals' (also known as 'The Wild Men,' 'the Highland Host,' or 'High Flyers'). The Evangelicals gained the majority, and they ruled with a heavy fist. They enacted Acts in the Assembly that were entirely beyond the power of a legally founded Church... The State refused to acknowledge their allegations. The strong arm of the law curtailed their excesses. They still held that their actions were authorized and necessary by the teaching of Christ's Headship, to which they ascribed particular and exceptional importance.'

Now, between 1838-1843, the State could not and would not allow these 'extravagances' in a State-paid Church. As a result, the Evangelical party seceded, claiming that "we are still the Church of Scotland, the only Church that deserves the name, the only Church that can be known and recognized by the maintaining of those principles to which the Church of our fathers was true when she was on the mountain and the field when she was under persecution when she was an outcast."

Thus, the Free Kirk was the Kirk, whereas the Established

Kirk was heretical, or as Knox would have put it, 'ane rotten Laodicean.' The Church of Scotland had been a Kirk established by law (or by what was said to be a legal Parliament) since August 1560, but had never, perhaps, for an hour attained its full ideal relation to the State; had never been granted its entire claims, but only so much or so little of these as the political situation compelled the State to concede, or enabled it to withdraw. There had always been Kirk members who claimed all that the Free Kirk demanded in 1843, but they never obtained nearly as much as they demanded; they frequently received much less than they desired, and no State could provide the whole amount of their aspirations to a State-paid Church. Only by separating the Church from the State could total independence be achieved. The Free Kirk broke away, but they maintained that they were the Church of Scotland and that the State had a responsibility to create and sustain them while providing them complete freedom.

In 1851, an Act and Declaration of the Free Kirk's Assembly stated: 'She holds still, and through God's grace will ever hold, that civil ruler must recognize the truth of God according to His word, and to promote and support the Kingdom of Christ without assuming any jurisdiction in it, or any power over it....'

If we may speak carnally, the state should pay the piper but not pretend to set the music.

Now we're getting close to the mystery: what was the difference between the Free Kirk and the United Presbyterians, who have been merged with that organization since 1900? The disagreement was that the Free Kirk believed it was the State's responsibility to create her and leave her in complete independence. Still, the United Presbyterians held the polar opposite view: the State cannot and must not create any Church or fund any Church out of national resources. So when the two Kirks merged in 1900, the Free Kirk either abandoned the belief about which she claimed in 1851 that "she maintains it yet, and by God's grace ever shall maintain it," or she saw it as a mere pious view that did not prohibit her from joining a Kirk with opposite principles. The small minority—the Wee Frees, today's Free Kirk—would not accept this compromise, 'therefore these tears,' to hide disagreements in fundamentally metaphysical doctrine.

Now, as we have indicated, the foundation of all the problems, all the schisms, and sorrows of more than three centuries resides in some of John Knox's beliefs, and one wonders what Kirk John Knox would be if he were living today. I believe the venerable Reformer would be found among the ranks of the Established Kirk, or 'the Auld Kirk.' He would not have gone into the wilderness in 1843, and he would have disagreed with the United Presbyterians' ideals. This notion may seem surprising at first look, but it was developed after many hours of careful thought.

To the extent that he ever reasoned them out, Knox's theories rested on this unassailable rock, namely, that Calvinism, as he regarded it, was definite in every detail. If the State, or "the civil magistrate," as he called it, agreed with

Knox, Knox was thrilled that the State should control religion. As it was in John Knox, the magistrate was to bring down Catholicism and other deviations from the truth with every possible tool of the law, including physical punishment, jail, exile, and death. If the State was ready and prepared to accomplish all of this, it was to be fully followed in religious issues. The authority in its hands was God-given—in reality, the State was the secular element of the Church. In this idealized view of the State, Knox talks on the magistrate's religious allegiance, in the style of what would be dubbed the strongest 'Erastianism' in this nation. The State 'rules the roast' in all things of religion and may, as Laud and Charles I., attempted, modify modes of worship—but only if the State completely agrees with the Kirk.

Thus, under Edward VI, Knox would have wished for the secular authority in England, the civil judge, to ban people from kneeling during the Sacrament's performance. That was perfectly within the State's jurisdiction, simply and only because Knox did not want people to kneel. However, when the civil judge insisted on people kneeling in Scotland long after Knox's death, supporters of Knox's principles disagreed that the judge (James VI.) had the jurisdiction to give such an order, and many refused to follow while staying inside the Established Church. They did not 'disrupt,' as the Free Church did; they just did what they liked and branded their loyal brothers as 'illegal pastors.' The eventual result was that they sparked the Civil War, with the famous Jenny Geddes firing the first shot, hurling her stool at the reader at St. Giles'. Thus, the

State was to be followed in issues of religion only when the State performed Kirk's bidding, and not otherwise. When he was originally hired as a 'licensed preacher' and State agent in England, Knox accepted as much of the State's liturgy as he chose; when the ritual required the people to kneel, Knox and his Berwick congregation resisted. He and the other royal priests, speaking before the King at Easter, condemned his ministers, Northumberland and the others, with equal openness. In his speech, Knox referred to them as Judas, Shebna, and other biblical villains. Later, he apologized for putting things so lightly; he should have addressed the ministers by their names, not cloaked things in a suggestion. In a sermon spoken before her, we cannot readily imagine a chaplain of her late Majesty, condemning the Chancellor of the Exchequer as 'Judas,' remark Mr. Gladstone. Nonetheless, Knox, a licensed preacher of a State Church, indulged his spiritual freedom' to that amount and felt ashamed that he had not gone further.

If this is 'Erastianism,' it is of a peculiar kind. Knox's opinion is that in a Catholic state, the ruler is not to be followed in religious issues by sincere believers; Knox said that the Catholic ruler should face 'passive opposition .' At other times, he should be murdered at sight. Over eighteen months, he expressed these many theories. In a Protestant nation, Catholics must follow the Protestant monarch or face imprisonment, exile, burning, and death. In a Protestant State, the Protestant monarch is to be followed in spiritual issues by Protestants. The extent that Kirk approves of his actions, or even further, in practice, if there is no likelihood of effective opposition.

If he had been living and still held his old principles in 1843, we may assume that Knox would not have left the Established Church for the Free Church since he did consent to numerous State rules that he did not approve of at the time. For example, he did not approve of bishops, and the Kirk created on his model in 1560 had no bishops. But, twelve years later, the State reintroduced bishops in the figure of the ruffian Regent Morton, and Knox did not withdraw to 'the mountain and the fields,' but made the most practical efforts to get the best conditions for the Kirk. He was elderly and worn out, yet he stayed in the Established Kirk and counseled no one to leave.

Again, as it was the Free Kirk's, it was his view that there should be no 'patronage,' no presenting ministers to cures by the patron. The congregations were to pick and 'call' any suitably qualified individual at their leisure, as they do today in all Kirks, including the Established Church (from 1874). However, throughout Knox's lifetime, the State overruled the Church's prerogative. Archibald Douglas, the most notorious criminal of the age, was given to the Kirk of Glasgow. The lords made numerous similar presents of evil and stupid cadets to prestigious livings. Morton made one of Riccio's killers a bishop! However, Knox did not advocate secession; rather, he suggested that non-residence, scandalous conduct, or erroneous theology on the part of the person submitted render his proposal 'invalid and of no force or effect, and this to take place likewise in the selection of the bishops.' As a result, Knox was a bit of an opportunist at times. If he had been living in 1843, he would have stayed in the Establishment and pushed to eliminate 'patronage,' which was achieved from inside in 1874. If this theory is correct, the Free Kirk was more Knoxian than John Knox and deviated from his norm. He was willing to give up a lot of spiritual independence' rather than split with the State. Many times, long after he died, the National Church, under duress, accepted concessions.

Knox understood the distinction between the ideal and the practical. It was ideal for all non-convertible Catholics to "die the death." But the ideal was never realized because the State was unwilling to assist the Kirk in this subject. It was perfect for any of 'the brothers,' aware of a vocation and sensing an opportunity, to treat an impenitent Catholic monarch as Jehu handled Jezebel. However, if any of the brothers had contacted Knox about the legality of assassinating Queen Mary in 1561-67, he would have discovered his error. He would have down the Reformer's steps far faster than he had climbed them.

Nonetheless, despite his willingness to compromise, Knox had a wonderfully mystical conception of the Kirk and its clergy. In his preface to The Judgment of the House of Lords, the editor of The Free Church Union Case, Mr. Taylor Innes (himself the author of a biography of the Reformer), writes: 'The Church of Scotland, as a Protestant Church, had its origin in the year 1560, for its first Confession dates from August and its first Assembly from December in that year.' In actuality, the Confession was recognized and approved as law in August 1560 by a very shaky legal Convention of the Estates. But Knox believed that the Protestant Church in, if not of, Scotland existed a year before that day and held 'the Keys' authority and, it would seem, 'the power of the Sword' before that day. The Protestant Church was 'a Church in existence' as soon as a local group of men of his views convened and picked a pastor and preacher who also administered the Sacraments. The Catholic Church, which had been formed by law at the time, was, according to Knox, no Church at all; her priests were not 'lawful ministers,' her Pope was the man of Sin ex officio, and the Church was 'the Kirk of the malignants'—'a lady of pleasure reared in Babylon.'

On the other hand, the true Church—even if it was just 200 men—was challenging the Kirk of the malignants, and it was the only one who was genuine. The State did not create and could not undo "the Trew Church," but it was obligated to build, develop, and obey it.

From 1559 until 1690, this final clause precipitated 130 years of violence, 'persecution,' and general discontent in Scotland. Why did the Kirk spend so much time 'in the heather,' hunting like a partridge on the field and the mountain? When Kirk's wilder spirits were not being persecuted, they were persecuting the State and tormenting the individual subject. All of this stemmed from Knox's conception of the Church. A small group of Calvinistic Protestants and a 'lawful preacher' were all that was required to form a Church. At first, little more than a 'call' to a preacher from a local group of Calvinistic Protestants was necessary to form a valid minister (eventually, significantly more was necessary). However, once the 'call' was granted and accepted, the notion held that the 'lawful minister' was superior to the State's rules as the legendary emperor was to grammar. A few 'lawful ministers' of this type possessed 'the power of the Keys;' they could excommunicate anyone and hand them over to Satan, and (apparently) they could present 'the power of the Sword' to any town council, which could then decree capital punishment against any Catholic priest who celebrated Mass, as he was required to do by State law. Knox's Kirk's moderate and fair requests in May 1559, before the Convention of Estates, ratified it in August 1560. It was because the wilder spirits among the pastors, rather than the Church, persisted in these assertions that the State, when given the opportunity, drove them into moors and mosses and hung quite a number of them.

I have never seen these circumstances completely described by any historian or biographer of Knox, save by the Reformer himself, partially in his History and partially in letters to a woman he knew. The riddle of the Kirks revolves around Knox's definition of the 'lawful minister' and his claim to absolute power.

To offer an example, Knox himself was a 'priest of the altar,' 'one of Baal's shaved type,' between 1540 and 1543. He then claimed nothing on that score. Following the assassination of Cardinal Beaton, the killers and their followers formed a congregation in the Castle of St. Andrews and asked Knox to be their preacher. He was now a 'legitimate minister.' In May 1559, he and four or five similarly legal pastors, two of whom were converted friars, one of whom was a baker, and one, Harlow, a tailor, joined forces with their Protestant supporters to burn the monasteries in Perth, as well as the altars and decorations of the church there. They immediately claimed 'the Keys' authority and threatened to excommunicate any friends who did not join them in arms. They, 'the brotherhood,' also opposed the death penalty for any priest who said Mass in Perth. The legitimate ministers could no longer contemplate hanging the priests themselves. They must have put 'the authority of the Sword' on the bellies and town council of Perth, I believe, since the Regent, Mary of Guise, removed these men from office when she invaded the town, which was considered as an illegal and perfidious move on her side. Again, in the summer of 1560, when Catholicism was still legal, the bellies of Edinburgh condemned the death sentence for obstinate Catholics. The Kirk also assigned legitimate pastors to some of the larger cities, establishing herself before the Estates recognized her in August 1560. Nothing could be more free and absolute than the Kirk in her early stages. On the other hand, even during Knox's lifetime, the State, having the upper hand under the Regent Morton, a strong man, introduced a modified kind of prelacy and patronage; did not restore to the Kirk her ' inheritance,'—the lands of the old

Church; and only hanged one priest, not improbably for a personal reason.

Thus, from the start, there was a conflict between the Protestant Church and the State. At different times, one preacher is believed to have stated that he was the lone 'lawful minister' in Scotland; and one of these persons, Mr. Cargill, excommunicated Charles II., while another, Mr Renwick, launched an assassination campaign against the Government. Both males were executed by hanging.

These were extreme claims of spiritual independence,' and the Kirk, or at least the majority of preachers, objected to such behavior, which may have been the logical extension of the idea of the 'lawful minister,' but was exceedingly uncomfortable in practice. Nevertheless, Kirk as a whole was devoted.

Sometimes the State, led by a powerful leader like Morton or James Stewart, Earl of Arran (a thoroughpaced ruffian), crushed the Church's pretensions. At times, as when Andrew Melville headed the Kirk under James VI., she asserted that there was only one monarch in Scotland, Christ and that the real King, the kid, James VI., was nothing more than 'Christ's stupid vassal.' In earthly affairs, he was paramount, but the Church's judicature was superior in spiritual things.

This seems to be completely reasonable, but who was to define what things were spiritual and which were temporal? The Kirk asserted the power to determine that matter; thus, it could spiritualize any issue of statesmanship, such as a royal marriage, commerce with Catholic Spain, which the Kirk prohibited, or the expulsion of Catholic peers. 'There is a judgment above yours, and that is God's; place it in the hands of the ministers, for we will judge the angels, said the apostle,' said the Rev. Mr. Pont to James VI. 'Ye shall sit upon twelve thrones and judge,' says Mr. Pont, referring to the apostles and, by extension, ministers.

In 1596, everything came to a head. The King asked officials of the Kirk if he might bring back certain earls who had been exiled for being Catholics provided they satisfied the Kirk.' He may not, according to the response. Knox had long argued that "a prophet" might teach treason (he is pretty specific about this) and that the prophet, as well as whoever carried out his teaching, would be innocent. At the time, a preacher was accused of preaching slanderously, and he refused to be tried by anybody other than his peers. What Court of Appeal could overturn the judgment of men who professed to 'judge angels' if they acquitted him, as they were morally guaranteed to do? A riot erupted in Edinburgh, and the King took his moment, gripped his nettle, the civic authorities supported him, and, in practice, the demands of real ministers provided little problem from then on until the foolishness of Charles I. led to the establishment of the Covenant. The Sovereign had overreached his powers as outrageously as the Kirk had, and the consequence was that the Kirk, now with the nobility and the people in arms on her side, was completely autocratic for roughly twelve years. Her crowning accomplishment was to successfully oppose the Estates in Parliament, leaving Scotland exposed to Cromwellian occupation. Noll accomplished what the Plantagenets and Tudors could not: he seized Scotland after the Kirk had paralyzed the State. The preachers discovered Cromwell to be a perfect 'Malignant,' refusing to allow prophets to preach treason or even let the General Assembly gathering. They could judge angels but not Ironsides; ex-communication and 'Kirk discipline' were frowned upon, and witches were seldom burnt. Cromwell said that the preachers 'had done their duty,' having discharged their bolt.

At this point, they broke into two factions: the Extremists, who referred to themselves as "the divine," and the men of a softer disposition.

During the Restoration, Charles II. should have sided with the softer group, some of whom were eager to have their ferocious colleagues exiled to Orkney, out of the way. But Charles's slogan was 'Never again .' He reinstated bishops without the despised liturgy via a pettifogging farce. After years of risings and suppressions, the ministers were forced to submit, receiving an 'indulgence' from the State. At the same time, only a few defenders of the clergy's ancient pretensions remained in the wildernesses of Southwestern Scotland. There may be three or four such ministers, or just one, but they, or he, were the only 'lawful ministers' in the eyes of 'the Remnant.' During the Revolution of 1688-89, the Remnant refused to accept the agreement that resulted in the re-establishment of the Presbyterian Kirk. They stood out, splintering into several sects; in 1847, the spiritual successors of the majority of them merged into a single organization known as 'The United Presbyterian Kirk.' The Moderates were in the majority in the Established Church until around 1837, when the inheritors of Knox's severe beliefs, which the majority of clergy rejected before the Revolution of 1688, gained the upper hand. They had placed their sort of ministers in the Highlands' most distant parishes, who drowned the votes of the Lowland Moderates in 1838, just as Highland 'Moderates' had drowned the votes of the Lowland Extremists under James VI. In 1843, most Extremists, or most of them, left the Kirk and formed the Free Kirk. When the Free Kirk joined the United Presbyterians in 1900, it was mostly Highland preachers who refused to accept the new union and today compose the true Free Kirk, or Wee Frees, with the endowments of the ancient Free Kirk of 1843. We can hardly say Beati possessors.

It has been shown, or I have attempted, erroneously or not, to show that, as wild and impossible as Knox's, Andrew Melville's, Mr. Pont's, and others' outstanding claims were, the old Scottish Kirk of 1560, by law established, was capable of giving up or suppressing these claims, even under Knox, and even while the Covenant remained in force. The majority of ministers were not irreconcilables after Charles II's return, before the Worcester war, before terrible Dunbar. By historical continuity, the Auld Kirk, the Kirk Established, has some right to call herself the Church of Scotland. In contrast, the opposing claimants, the men of 1843, appear to be descended from people like young Renwick, the last hero who died for their ideas, but not the only 'lawful minister' between Tweed and Cape Wrath. Other times, other methods.' All the Kirks are perfectly loyal; now none persecutes; interference with private life, 'Kirk discipline,' is at an all-time low; and, but for this recent 'parboil,' as our old writers put it, we might have said that, despite differences in terminology, all the Kirks are finally united in the only union worth having, that of peace and goodwill. That connection, let us hope, may be restored by good temper and common reason, traits that have not hitherto been prominent in the religious history of Scotland or England.

THE CONSPIRACY OF GOWRIE

The bizarre events known as 'The Gowrie Conspiracy' or 'The Slaying of the Ruthvens' unfolded in the following way, based on evidence that no one denies. On August 5, 1600, the King, James VI., left the stables at the House of Falkland to shoot a deer when the Master of Ruthven rode up and asked the king a question. Then, around seven o'clock in the morning, something happened. The Master was nineteen years old and lived with his brother, the Earl of Gowrie, who was twenty-two, in the family townhome in Perth, some twelve or fourteen miles from Falkland. After the conversation, the King pursued the hounds, and the 'long and painful' pursuit culminated in a kill near Falkland at around eleven o'clock. The King and the Master then rode to Perth, accompanied by around fifteen members of the Royal escort, including the Duke of Lennox and the Earl of Mar. Others from the King's company joined them; the total number may have been as few as twenty-five.

When they arrived in Perth, it seemed that they had not been anticipated. The Earl having eaten at noon, the Royal supper was delayed until two o'clock, and after the meager meal, the King and Master went upstairs alone. In contrast, the Earl of Gowrie led Lennox and others into his garden at the rear of the house, bordering on the Tay. While they were eating cherries, a Gowrie servant, Thomas Cranstoun (brother of Sir John of that ilk), received word that the King had already mounted and galloped out through the Inch of Perth. Gowrie requested horses, but Cranstoun informed him that his horses were two miles away in Scone, over the Tay. The gentlemen then walked to the house's street entrance, where the keeper informed them that the King had not ridden away. Gowrie lied to him, re-entered the home, went upstairs, and returned to persuade Lennox that James had left. All of this is proven on the stand by Lennox, Mar, Lindores, and a slew of other witnesses.

While the group remained outside the gate, a tower window above them opened, and the King emerged, angry, yelling 'Treason!' and pleading with Mar for assistance. Mar, along with Lennox and the majority of the others, rushed to the rescue up the home's main staircase, where they were met with a closed door that they couldn't open. Gowrie had not gone with his guests to help the King; instead, he was waiting in the street, wondering, 'What is the matter?' When two members of the King's household, Thomas and James Erskine, sought to capture him, the 'treason was committed beneath Gowrie's own home. His companions drove the Erskines away, and several Murrays from Tullibardine who were in Perth for a wedding encircled him. Gowrie fled, pulled a pair of 'twin swords,' and made his way inside his house's courtyard, joined by Cranstoun and others. They discovered the corpse of a guy lying at the foot of a short dark stairway, either injured or dead. Cranstoun dashed up the dimly lit stairwell, followed by Gowrie, two Ruthvens, Hew Moncrieff, Patrick Eliot, and maybe more. They discovered Sir Thomas Erskine, a crippled Dr. Herries, a young gentleman of the Royal Household named

John Ramsay, and Wilson, a servant, with drawn swords at the top of the short spiral stair. Cranstoun was injured, and he and his comrades left, abandoning Gowrie, who had been run through the body by Ramsay. All the time, the other door of the long Gallery Chamber rang with the hammer blows of Lennox and his crew while the town bell summoned the residents. Erskine and Ramsay had now shut the door opening on the tiny stairwell, which the retainers of Gowrie had hit with axes. The King's party forced the lock and entered Lennox, Mar, and the rest of the King's entourage by using a hamper delivered to them through a hole in the other door of the gallery. They allowed James out of a tiny turret opening from the Gallery Chamber, and after some disputes with the enraged mob and Perth's magistrates, they took the King to Falkland after dark.

The end consequence was the deaths of Gowrie and his brother, the Master (whose corpse was found at the bottom of the tiny stairway), as well as Ramsay, Dr. Herries, and several of Gowrie's retainers.

The killing of the Master of Ruthven was described as follows: "When James yelled 'Treason!' from the stable door, young Ramsay heard his voice but not his words." He'd hurried into the quadrangle, dashed up the tight steps, discovered a door behind which a fight could be heard, 'dang in' the door, and seen the King battling with the Master. Behind them stood a guy, the center of the enigma, to which he paid no attention. Instead, he drew his sword, cut the Master across the face and neck, and shoved him downstairs. Ramsay immediately appealed to Sir Thomas Erskine from the window, who, together with Herries and Wilson, rushed to his aid, murdered the injured Master, and imprisoned James (who had no weapon) in the turret. Then there was the battle in which Gowrie died. Except for a townsman who subsequently retracted his testimony, no one saw the mystery man on the tower again.

The entire thing was observed by the King's troops, the retainers of Gowrie, and several Perth civilians. There was no trace of Gowrie and his party's scheme or scheme. His supporters claimed that he intended to depart Perth that day for 'Lothian,' that is, for his castle at Dirleton, near North Berwick, where he had despatched most of his soldiers and foodstuffs. They stated James had asked the Master to meet him at Falkland, and Gowrie had never expected the Master to return with the King.

James's version was given in a public letter written to the King's dictation at Falkland by David Moysie, a notary, on the night of the events, which we only know about through the report of Nicholson, the English resident at Holyrood (August 6). Nicholson only repeated what Elphinstone, the secretary, told him about the contents of the letter, written to the King's dictation at Falkland by David Moysie, a not At the end of August, James prepared and distributed a detailed narrative that was almost similar to Nicholson's account of Elphinstone's description on the contents of the August 5

Falkland letter.

The King's story is widely believed until we get to the point when he talks with Alexander Ruthven in Falkland before the buck-hunt begins. There was such an interview, which lasted approximately a quarter of an hour, but only James understood what it was about. He claims that after an exceptionally low obeisance, Ruthven told him the following story:—While walking alone in the meadows outside Perth the previous evening, he saw 'a base-like guy, unknown to him, with a cloak, draped around his lips,' a standard measure to prevent identification. When asked who he was and what his mission was 'in such a lonesome region, being remote from all means,' the man was taken aback. Ruthven apprehended him and discovered "a large, broad pot, all full of coined gold in huge bits" under his arm. Ruthven transported the guy to Perth and put him in a 'privy darned house'—that is, a room— while keeping the secret to himself. He left Perth at 4 a.m. to inform the King, encouraging him to 'take order' in the situation immediately since Lord Gowrie was unaware of it. When James argued it was none of his concern since the gold was not a treasure trove, Ruthven labeled him 'too scrupulous,' adding that his brother, Gowrie, 'and other important men,' may intervene. James then inquired about the money and their bearer, assuming that the gold was foreign, smuggled in by Jesuits for Catholic insurgents. Ruthven responded that the bearer seemed to be a previously unknown 'Scots guy' and that the gold seemed foreign mintage. As a result, James was convinced that the gold was foreign, and the carrier disguised Scots priest. As a result, he recommended sending back with Ruthven a retainer of his own, accompanied by a warrant to Gowrie, then Provost of Perth, and the Bailies, to seize the man and the money. Ruthven said that if they did, the money would be wasted and pleaded with the King to ride over immediately, be 'the first seer,' and award him 'at his honorable discretion.'

The weirdness of the story and the weirdness of Ruthven's demeanor astounded James, who answered that he would respond after the search was ended. Ruthven speculated that the guy would make a disturbance and uncover the entire thing, leading the riches to be tampered with. Gowrie would miss him, yet Gowrie and the townspeople would be 'at the preaching if James arrived immediately.' James remained silent and followed the dogs. Still, he meditated on the narrative, and he was summoned.

Ruthven and promised to accompany him to Perth soon after the quest was over.

In this section, James explains that, though he was unaware that any man was with Ruthven, he did have two friends, one of whom, Andrew Henderson, now sent to Gowrie, instructing him to prepare supper for the King. This is not direct proof from James. He was unaware and unconcerned that any guy alive had arrived with Ruthven.

Ruthven was constantly close to the King throughout the pursuit, pressing him to 'hurry the finish of the hunting.' The buck was killed near the stables, and Ruthven refused to let James wait for a second horse: dispatched after him. So the king didn't even linger to 'brittle' the deer, instead of informing the Duke of Lennox, Mar, and others that he was riding to Perth to consult with Gowrie and would return before sunset. Some of the Court proceeded to Falkland to get new horses, while others followed slowly with tired steeds. They followed 'unwanted by him,' since there was the word that the King was about to seize the harsh Master of Oliphant. Ruthven pleaded with James not to send Lennox and Mar, but merely three or four slaves, to which the King replied: "half furiously."

James was suspicious of this unusual behavior. He'd known Ruthven, who was vying for the position of Gentleman of the Bedchamber, or Cubicular. 'The furthest that the King's suspicion could go was, that it may be that the Earl, his brother, had treated him so harshly that the young gentleman, being of a high spirit, had taken such displeasure that he was over himself;' hence his strange, disturbed, and melancholy behavior. While they were riding, James checked his phone.

Lennox, whose first wife was Gowrie's sister. Lennox had never seen anything like mental instability in young Ruthven. Still, James ordered the Duke to 'accompanies him into that dwelling' (chamber), where the money and its carrier lay. Lennox believed the gold tale was 'unlikely.' Ruthven, observing them conversing, advised James to be discreet and bring no one with him to the initial examination of the riches.

As a result, the King rode onward 'between trust and mistrust.' Ruthven sent his second friend, Andrew Ruthven, to Gowrie about two miles from Perth. Ruthven galloped ahead of the rest of the party when they were within a mile of Perth. Gowrie was at supper, having ignored the two previous messengers.

Gowrie met James 'near the end of the Inch,' with fifty or sixty men; the Royal entourage was then of fifteen people, with swords only, and no daggers or 'whingers.' Dinner did not materialize for another hour (say 2 p.m.). James whispered to Ruthven that he needed to view the riches right now; Ruthven advised him to wait and not attract Gowrie's suspicions by whispering ('rounding'). As a result, James focused his chat on Gowrie, receiving "only half words and poor phrases" from him. ' When it was time for dinner, Gowrie stood pensively beside the King's table, frequently talking to the servants, 'and oft-times walked in and out,' as he did before supper. The suite waited about, as was customary until James was ready to eat when Gowrie brought them to their separate table in the hall; 'he sat not down with them as the normal fashion is,' but remained quietly by the King, who bantered him 'in a homely fashion.'

Having sat for too long, Ruthven murmured to James that he longed to be free of him.

Because Ruthven had requested it, James dispatched Gowrie into the hall to present a type of grace-cup to the suite, as was customary. James then stood to join Ruthven, requesting that Sir Thomas Erskine accompany him. Ruthven urged that James 'order openly' that no one follows at once, pledging that 'he should make anyone or two follow that he liked to call for.'

The King then proceeded alone with Ruthven past the end of the hall, up a staircase, and past three or four apartments, Ruthven 'ever shutting behind him every door as he went,' anticipating attendants who never arrived since Ruthven never requested them. We don't know if James saw the doors lock or deduced it from the subsequent revelation that one door was locked. Then Ruthven presented a more cheerful smile than he had all day, always stating that he had him sure and secure enough guarded. ' Finally, they arrived at 'a tiny study' (a turret room), where James discovered 'not a bondman, but a freeman, with a dagger at his waist and a most abased visage.' Ruthven shut the turret door, pulled the man's dagger, and pointed it at the King's breast, 'avowing now that the King behooved to be in his will and used as the list,' threatening death if James shouted out or opened the window. He also reminded the King of the loss of his father, the late Gowrie (executed for treason in 1584). In a while, the other guy was 'trembling and quaking.' James launched into a lengthy rant on various topics, vowing forgiveness and quiet provided Ruthven immediately let him go. Ruthven then revealed the truth and assured James that his life would be securely provided he remained silent; the rest Gowrie would explain. Then, instructing the other guy to guard the King, he left, closing the door behind him. He'd made James vow not to open the window. In his short absence, James learned from the armed guy that he had just lately been locked up in the turret for reasons he didn't understand. James told him to open the window with his 'right hand.' The guy did what he was told.

The King's narration reverts to a subject outside of his perception here (the events which occurred downstairs during his absence). Many aristocrats and gentlemen have sworn under oath to substantiate his story. He claims (and we repeat what we said before) that, while he was absent, as his train was rising from supper, one of the Earl's servants, Cranstoun, hurried in swiftly, telling the Earl that the King had gotten on a horse, and 'was going across the Inch' (isle) of Perth. The Earl informed the nobility, and they all went to the gate. The porter reassured them that the King had not left the palace. Gowrie told the porter a falsehood but then turned to Lennox and Mar and claimed he'd obtain further information. He then raced back across the court and upstairs, returning hurriedly with the news that 'the King had gone, long ago, via the rear gate, and would not be overtaken unless they hastened.'

On their way to the stables for their horses, the aristocrats had to pass through the tower's window on the first level, where James was imprisoned. Ruthven had returned at this point, 'throwing his hands about in a frenzied fashion as a man lost.' He then sought to tie the royal hands with his garter, declaring no remedy for it and that the King had to die. During the battle, James dragged Ruthven towards the previously open window. When the King's companions were waiting on the street below, with Gowrie among them, James yelled for aid, 'holding out the right side of his head and his right elbow.' Gowrie stood 'always wondering what it meant,' but as we saw, Lennox, Mar, and others rushed in and up the main staircase to locate the King.

Meanwhile, James forced Ruthven out of the tower, 'the said Mr. Alexander's head under his arms, and himself on his knees,' towards the room door that led to the dark stairway. 'The other gentleman is doing nothing but standing behind the King's back and shivering all the while,' James was attempting to gain hold of Ruthven's sword and draw it. A young gentleman of the Royal Household, John Ramsay, arrived from the dark rear staircase at this time and struck Ruthven with his knife. 'The other guy backed out. James then forced Ruthven down the rear steps, where he was killed by Sir Thomas Erskine and Dr. Herries, who were approaching from that direction. The remainder of the story began with Gowrie's death. James's return to Falkland was delayed for two or three hours due to a riot among the townspeople.

This is the published version of the King's story. It corresponds closely with the letter sent to Cecil by Nicholson, the English agent, on August 6.

On August 5, James had his version, from which he never deviated, ready. Only one conclusion can be taken from his story. Gowrie and his brother had attempted to get James to their home when he was practically unsupervised. They had an armed guy on the turret who would help the Master grab the King. The scheme was thwarted when James was well attended, the armed man turned coward, and Gowrie falsely declared the King's departure to have his entourage follow back to Falkland and so leave the King in the hands of his captors. The conspiracy could not be abandoned after it was planned since the plotters had no prisoner with a pot of money to deliver. Thus their intended treason would have been obvious.

How well does James' story hold up? At the Ruthvens' postmortem trial in November, witnesses such as Lennox testified to a quarter-hour conversation with Ruthven at Falkland before the hunt. The early arrival of Andrew Henderson to Gowrie's residence, at half-past ten, is attested to by two gentlemen called Hay and one called Moncrieff, who was then with Gowrie on business, to which he immediately refused to attend further, in the case of the Hays. A manuscript vindication of the Ruthvens further supports Henderson's attendance in Falkland released at the time. None of the King's party saw him, and their failure to testify that they did see him demonstrates their honesty. Thus, Gowrie arranged no supper for the King, despite Henderson's early arrival with word of his impending visit, demonstrating that Gowrie intended to seem surprised. Again, Henderson's travel on the night of August 5 demonstrates that he was involved: why else would a guy travel who had not been seen by anybody (save a Perth witness who retracted his testimony) connected with the terrible events? Except for a few of Gowrie's retainers who actively participated in the conflict, no one else escaped.

The Kingside with Ruthven in a dispute over ownership of the church lands of Scone, which Gowrie owned and Ruthven coveted, explains James' notion that Ruthven was crazy as a result of brutal treatment by his brother Gowrie. This is referenced lightly in a current document. [13] Again, Lennox testified under oath that James told him the tale of the lure, the pot of gold, as they rode to Perth. Lennox was an honorable guy who had married Gowrie's sister.

On his way back to Gowrie's home, Ruthven informed a retainer, Craigingelt, that he'd been on an errand not far distant,' and explained the King's appearance by claiming he'd been 'brought' by the royal saddler to collect payment of a debt to the man. However, now that James has granted Gowrie a year's protection from creditor pursuit, there is no evidence of the saddler's presence. Ruthven had lied to Craigingelt; he had been at Falkland, not 'on an errand not far away.'

Cranstoun, Gowrie's man, confirmed bringing the news, or rumor, of the King's departure. On oath, Lennox, Lindores, Ray (a magistrate of Perth), the porter himself, and others established that Gowrie went inside the house to check the truth; urged that it was real; spoke the lie to the porter, who denied it; and sought to have the King's company take a horse and follow.

The fact that the King was trapped behind a door that

couldn't be broken open is undeniable.

All of these are facts that cannot be denied. However, they were called into question when Henderson, Gowrie's factor or steward and a Perth town councilor, emerged from hiding between August 11 and August 20, narrated his tale, and admitted to being the man on the turret. On the night of August 4, he said that Gowrie ordered him to ride to Falkland with the Master of Ruthven and return with any message that Ruthven may convey. When the Hays and Moncrieff spotted him, he returned with word that the King was on his way. An hour later, Gowrie told him to put on a mail shirt and plate sleeves because he would arrest a Highlander in the Shoe-gait. Later, when the King arrived, Henderson was sent to Ruthven in the gallery and ordered to perform whatever was requested. Ruthven then locked him up in the turret without explaining why. The King was eventually taken inside the turret, and Henderson claims that, to a little measure, he calmed Ruthven's fury. During Ramsay and Ruthven's fight, he crept downstairs, went home, and escaped that night.

Henderson's presence at Falkland was disputed at all. Nobody attested to his being there, but it is acknowledged by the modern apologist, who accuses the King of organizing the whole plot against the Ruthvens. Even though the courtyard was full, no one saw Henderson slink away from the tight stairwell. However, one Robertson, a Perth notary, testified (September 23) that he saw Henderson slip out of the tiny stairway and walk over the Master's corpse; Robertson called to him, but he did not respond. If Robertson lied on September 23, he withdrew, or rather, withheld, his testimony during the November trial. If he had stuck to his earlier declaration, his life would not have been worth living in Perth, where the people supported the Ruthvens. In the lack of additional witness, several tales spread about Henderson's departure from Perth during the day, as well as his presence in the kitchen during the crisis. He was last seen at the house right before the King's supper, and according to his version, the Master shut him up in the tower. Robertson's initial story was most likely accurate. Other witnesses denied seeing Gowrie's retainers, who were undoubtedly present during the quadrangle brawls to protect their neighbors. Henderson never explained why he bolted so quickly if he wasn't the guy on the turret. As a result, I believe that his tale is mostly genuine since he was at Falkland and returned early.

Given all of this, only one of two hypotheses is viable. The incident was not by chance; James did not panic and yell 'Treason!' out the window just because he found himself alone in a turret—and why in a remote turret?—with the Master. The gallery's closed door is an effective response to such an argument. Someone had it locked for some reason. As a result, either the Ruthvens conspired against the King or the King conspired against the Ruthvens. As we will see, both sides had fair reasons for hatred—that is, Gowrie and James had reasons to dispute; but with the young Master, whose cause, as concerns the lands of Scone, the King championed, he had no reason to be angry. How did James manage his fascination if he was guilty?

Let us imagine the King sets his scheme with reasons to despise Gowrie. He selects a day when he knows the Murrays of Tullibardine will be in Perth for one of the clan's weddings. They will protect the King against the townspeople, who are customers of their Provost, Gowrie.

James then invites Ruthven to Falkland (as Ruthven's defense claimed): he comes at the unusually early hour of 6.30 a.m. However, James has already concocted the pot of gold narrative to be said to Lennox as evidence that Ruthven is bringing him to Perth—that he has not invited Ruthven.

Next, by quietly disseminating rumors that he intends to seize the Master of Oliphant, James gets a large train of retainers, say twenty-five men without guns, while avoiding the suspicion that would be raised if he commanded them to follow him. Finally, James has decided to sacrifice Ruthven (with whom he has no beef) only as bait to lure Gowrie into a trap.

Having deceived Lennox into joining Ruthven alone in the mansion of Gowrie, James covertly prepares for Ruthven to discreetly ask him or Erskine to follow upstairs, intending to provoke Ruthven into a treasonable attitude just as they come on the scene. He predicts that Lennox, Erskine, or both would knife Ruthven without hesitation and that Gowrie would run forward to avenge his brother and be slaughtered.

His Majesty's well-planned scheme falls apart on the surface when Ruthven summons neither Lennox nor Erskine for reasons best known to himself. Observing this condition, James quickly and effectively remodels his strategy. He does not begin to cause the brawl until, for whatever reason, he is in the turret and hears his train conversing outside on the street. He had foreseen their appearance by instructing a servant of his own to propagate the false word of his departure, which Cranstoun had brought innocently. Why did the King do this, given that his initial plan did not need such a ruse? He had also convinced Gowrie to believe the tale despite the porter's rejection of its feasibility and stick with it while making no meaningful effort to confirm its veracity. Making Gowrie do this instead of carefully inspecting the home is undoubtedly the King's most spectacular and unexplained achievement.

As a result, the King has two strings to his malicious bow. The first was that Ruthven would fetch Erskine and Lennox on his instructions, and when they arrived, James would goad Ruthven into a treasonable attitude, after which Lennox and Erskine would dirk him. If this failed (which it did since Ruthven did not heed instructions), the second strategy was to trick Gowrie into bringing the retinue beneath the tower window, where the King could open the window and yell 'Treason!' as soon as he heard their voices and footfall below. This strategy is successful. James screams through the window. He had somehow sealed the entrance leading into the gallery while giving Ramsay a signal to wait outside the house, within earshot, and come up via the rear staircase constructed in a visible tower.

The rest is simple. Gowrie is free to bring up as many men as he wants. Still, Ramsay has been given orders to horrify him by claiming that the King has been slain (this was alleged) and then to run him through as he gives ground or drops his points; this after a decent form of resistance in which three of the King's four men are wounded.

'Master of the human heart,' like Lord Bateman, James understands that Ruthven will not just abandon him when provoked by insult and that Gowrie will not just stand in the street and call the townspeople when he learns of his brother's death.

To acquire a witness to the reality of his fraudulent account of events, James must have begun by ingeniously persuading Henderson, Gowrie's steward, either to flee and then return later with evidence or to be present in the turret and then flee. Perhaps the King uttered his man-in-the-turret story only 'in the air,' and Henderson, having fled in fright, later sees money in it,' and reappears with a series of lies. Aristotle says, 'Chance loves Art,' and chance may easily favor an artist as competent and moral as his Majesty. To be sure, Mr. Hill Burton claims that "the hypothesis that the entire thing was a Court plan to destabilize the mighty House of Gowrie must be discounted at immediately, after a calm weighing of the facts, as being outside the realm of logical conclusions." Those who formed it had to put one of the very last men in the world to accept such a fate in the position of an unarmed man who, without any preparation, was to render himself into the hands of his armed adversaries and cause a succession of surprises and acts of violence, which he would rule to a determined and preconcerted plan by his courage and skill.'

Without a strategy, James intended to start a quarrel and 'go it blind if there was a royal conspiracy.' This, however, goes much beyond the King's usual and amorous rashness. We must favor the notion of a finely coordinated and well-executed plan, built with alternatives so that if one thread breaks, another will hold tight. That strategy has been outlined to the best of my ability. To use an ironic phrase, everything of this notion is utterly unbelievable. James was not the kind of wildly daring individual who would go weaponless with Ruthven, who carried a sword and provoke him into arrogance. Even if he had been bold, the scheme is of such intricacy that no sane man, much alone a fearful guy, could concoct and carry out a scheme that is at the mercy of many unforeseeable variables. Assume the Master is dead, and Gowrie is a free man on the street. He merely had to sound the tocsin, gather his dedicated townspeople, surround the house, and gently request answers.

Take, for example, the hypothesis of Gowrie's guilt. The motivations for evil intent on either side may be simply outlined below. The Ruthvens had been the Crown's adversaries since the assassination of Riccio (1566). Gowrie's grandfather and father were leaders in the assault on Mary and Riccio; Gowrie's father humiliated Queen Mary by romantic attempts when imprisoned in Loch Leven Castle, she claims. In 1582, Gowrie's father kidnapped James and imprisoned him in deplorable conditions. He escaped and reunited with his jailer, who plotted again and was executed in 1584, while the Ruthven lands were forfeited. The Ruthvens were restored by a new revolution (1585-1586). In July 1593, Gowrie's mother, via a cunning ambush, allowed the Earl of Bothwell to abduct the King once again. Our Gowrie, being a youngster, joined Bothwell in open rebellion in 1594. He was pardoned and traveled abroad in August 1594, traveling as far as Rome, studying at Padua, and returning to England in March 1600, beckoned by the Kirk party. Elizabeth pampered him here, and he was then on practically warlike terms with James. For thirty years, Elizabeth had supported every treason of the Ruthvens, and Cecil had aided and abetted several attempts to seize James. As late as April 1600, these plots were plentiful. The goal was always to establish Kirk's supremacy over the King, and Gowrie, as the natural noble head of the Kirk, was summoned to Scotland in 1600 by the Rev. Mr. Bruce, the head of the political preachers whom James had controlled in 1596-97. When Gowrie arrived, he immediately took command of the Opposition and successfully opposed the King's request for supplies, which had been necessitated by his unfriendly ties with England, on June 21, 1600. Gowrie then left the Court and went hunting in Atholl about July 20, leaving his mother (who had previously enticed James into a trap) at his Perth home. On August 1, Gowrie informed his mother of his impending homecoming. She proceeded to the family stronghold of Dirleton, between North Berwick and the sea, while Gowrie arrived at his Perth home on August 3, with the understanding that he would ride to Dirleton on August 5. He had sent the majority of his soldiers and supplies there. We know he embarked on a longer adventure on August 5.

We've established that James' storyline is fantastic. Aside from the overall character of the events and the peculiar behavior of himself and his brother, there is no evidence to support a conspiracy by Gowrie. But, if he plotted, he was only carrying out the usual strategy of his grandparents, father, mother, and comrade, Bothwell, who was at the time in exile in Spain, ripening a conspiracy in which he claimed Gowrie as one of his confederates. Gowrie could not expect to rouse the disgruntled Barons or emancipate the preachers who had called him home while the King was still a free man. Instead, allow the King to flee, and Kirk's party, the English side, would prevail.

The implication is that the King was made to vanish, and Gowrie agreed to do so. Mr. Cowper, minister of Perth, and Mr. Rhynd, Gowrie's former teacher, testified that he was used to speaking of the necessity for absolute concealment 'in the accomplishment of a noble and perilous aim.' Such a goal as the capture of the King by a surprise onslaught was customary in Scottish politics. Cecil's records from this time and after that are replete with similar proposals presented by Scottish explorers. So it's no surprise that two guys as young as the Ruthvens would devise such a passionate and risky scheme.

Its initial intention must assess the scheme: to lure James to Perth at an early hour of the day with just two or three servants. If the King had visited Gowrie House early and sparsely attended, he might have been taken through Fife, disguised, in the procession of Gowrie as he traveled to Dirleton. From there, he might be transported by sea to Fastcastle, the impenetrable eyrie of Gowrie's and Bothwell's old friend, Logan of Restalrig. I have proven by comparison of handwritings that the famous letters considered by Scott, Tytler, and Hill-Burton as evidence of that conspiracy were all faked. Still, one of them, claimed by the forger as his model for the others, is, I believe, a fake copy of a real original. In that letter (to Gowrie), Logan is persuaded to compare their strategy to one devised against a "nobleman of Padua," where Gowrie had studied. This comment, in a postscript, cannot have been made up by the forger, Sprot, a low country attorney, and Logan's creation. The other letters are just variations on the melody established by this composition.

A scheme of this kind is not feasible, unlike the unbelievable conspiracy claimed to James. The concept was only one of several of its like that were continually being invented at the time. The next-to-impossible scenario is that Ruthven left Henderson, as he said, on the turret without tutoring in his role. The King's party did not think Henderson was telling the truth; he had accepted the role but turned cowardly, they said. This is especially plausible given that, in December 1600, a gentleman called Robert Oliphant, a servant of Gowrie, escaped from Edinburgh, where some admissions blabbed by him had gained public attention. He had claimed that Gowrie had persuaded him to play the armed man in the turret in Paris early in 1600; that he had 'with good cause dissuaded him; that the Earl after that left him and negotiated with Henderson in that matter; that Henderson attempted it and yet fainted'—that is, became craven. Though the Privy Council acquitted Oliphant of hiding treason nine years later in England, had he not departed from Edinburgh in December 1600, the whole case may have been made apparent since witnesses were then available.

We conclude that, because there was undoubtedly a Ruthven plot, and because the King could not have invented and carried out the affair, and because Gowrie, the leader of the Kirk party, was young, romantic, and 'Italianate,' he did plan a device of the regular and usual kind, but was frustrated, and fell into the pit which he had dug. Still, the Presbyterians would never accept that the youthful head of the Kirk party tried, and considerably more regularly plotted to do, what the godly leaders had often done, and considerably more often plotted to do, with Cecil and Elizabeth's full permission. The conspiracy was orthodox, but historians with Presbyterian and Liberal leanings assume that the King was the conspirator. The Ruthvens were long mourned, and women in Perthshire chanted to their babies, 'Sleep ye, sleep ye, my bonny Earl o' Gowrie,' even in the nineteenth century.

A woman has even written to tell me that she is a descendent of the younger Ruthven, who fled to England after being stabbed by Ramsay and Erskine, married, and had a family. I answered in vain that young Ruthven's corpse had been embalmed, shown in the Scottish Parliament, and chopped to bits, which were put on spikes in public locations, and that he was unlikely to marry after these ordeals. Nevertheless, the lady's faith was not to be shaken.

Mr. Edmund Gosse acknowledges Ramsay the Ruthven killer as the author of a Century of English Sonnets (1619), of which Lord Cobham holds an individual copy in The Atheneum for August 28, 1902. Réné Giffart published the book in Paris. Gifford's Scottish name was spelled 'Giffart,' indicating that the publisher was of Scottish heritage.

THE MYSTERY OF CAMPDEN

The average historical riddle is at least evident enough that one of two answers must be correct, if only we knew which. Perkin Warbeck was either the true King or an imposter. Giacomo Stuardo of Naples (1669) was Charles II's oldest son or charlatan. Mattioli or Eustache Dauger was undoubtedly the Man in the Iron Mask. Gowrie plotted against James VI., or James VI. plotted against Gowrie, and so on. These riddles are motivated by logic and human nature. But, save for one idea, there is no sparkle of reason or rational human nature at the heart of the Campden riddle. The happenings seem to be as random as those in a restless dream. 'The Whole Matter is dark and mysterious; which we must therefore leave to Him who alone knows all Things, in His rightful Time, to expose and bring to Light.'

According to the author of 'A True and Perfect Account of the Examination, Confession, Trial, and Execution of Joan Perry, and her two sons, John and Richard Perry, for the Supposed Murder of Will Harrison, Gent., Being One of the most extraordinary Occurrences that has transpired in the Memory of Man,' Sent in a letter to Thomas Shirly, Doctor of Physick, in London (by Sir Thomas Overbury, of Burton, in the County of Gloucester, Knt., and one of his Majesty's Justices of the Peace). Also, Mr. Harrison's account,' and so forth. (London: Printed for John Atkinson in St. Paul's Church-Yard, near the Chapter House. But, unfortunately, there is no date, although it seems to be 1676.)

Such is the wide and breathless title of a treatise that, by undeserved good fortune, has been published.

I'm lucky; I just bought it. Sir Thomas Overbury, 'the unfortunate victim of the evil Countess of Somerset' (who had the older Overbury poisoned in the Tower), was the Justice of the Peace who functioned as Juge d'Instruction in the case of Harrison's abduction, according to Mr. John Paget.

To get to the point of the narrative. At 1660, William Harrison, Gent., was steward or "factor" to the Viscountess Campden in Chipping Campden, Gloucestershire, a single-street village nestled in the Cotswold hills. The lady did not dwell at Campden House, which its owner burned down during the Great Rebellion to spite the rebels, much as its Jacobite ruler burned down castle Tirrim during the '15. Instead, Harrison lived in a section of the building that had not been destroyed. He had been a servant of the Hickeses and Campdens for fifty years, was seventy years old (which adds to the mystery), was married, and had children, including Edward, his oldest son.

Mr. Harrison's home was broken into at high noon on a market day in 1659, while he and his whole family were 'at the Lecture,' at church, a Puritan method of edifying. A ladder had been propped up against the wall, the bars of a second-story window had been yanked away with a plowshare (which had been left in the chamber), and 140 l. of Lady Campden's money had been taken. The thief was never apprehended, which is unusual in such a tiny and isolated community.

However, the times had changed, and a roaming Cavalier or Roundhead soldier may have 'cracked the crib.' Perry, Harrison's servant, was heard pleading for aid in the garden a few weeks later. He displayed a hacked-handled sheep-pick,' declaring that he had been attacked by two guys in white with bare swords and had defended himself with his primitive instrument. It is strange that Mr. John Paget, a sharp-witted writer who served as a police judge in Hammersmith for many years, mentions nothing about the heist of 1659 or Perry's insane behavior in the garden. Perry's actions there and his hysterical creation of the two armed guys in white reveal a lot about his personality. Of course, the two guys in white were never found, but we subsequently encounter three individuals who are no less obnoxious and much more strange. They seemed to be three men in buckram.'

In any case, even the unadventurous had experiences in peaceful Campden. They reached a climax the next year, on August 16, 1660. Harrison got up early (?) and traveled the two miles to Charringworth to collect his lady's rentals. The fall day was drawing in, and between eight and nine o'clock, old Mrs. Harrison sent her servant, John Perry, to meet his master on his way home. In Harrison's window, lights were also left on. That night, neither master nor man returned. It is curious that the younger Harrison, Edward, did not look for his father until very early the following morning: he had the advantage of a late-rising moon for nocturnal searching. In the morning, Edward saw Perry, returning alone: he had not located his master. The couple proceeded to Ebrington, a hamlet halfway between Campden and Charringworth, and discovered that Harrison had visited at the residence of one Daniel on the previous evening as he made his way home via Ebrington. The time is not specified, but Harrison vanished just past Ebrington, less than a mile from Campden. Next, Edward and Perry learned that a poor lady had found a hat, band, and comb belonging to Harrison on the route outside Ebrington, amid some whins or furze; they were discovered within approximately half a mile of his own home. The band was bloodied, and the cap and comb had been slashed and cut. Please take note of the exact words of Sir Thomas Overbury, the judge who presided over the preliminary examinations: 'The Hat and Comb were slashed and chopped, and the Band bloodied, but nothing more could be discovered.' As a result, the hat and comb were not on Harrison's head when they were chopped and chopped; otherwise, they would have been blood-stained; the band around the neck was bloody, but there was no evidence of blood on the road. This paragraph contains the solution to the riddle.

When word of the finding of these things spread, everyone raced to look for Harrison's body, which they did not locate.

An older man like Harrison was unlikely to remain at Charringworth very late, but whatever happened on the roadway seems to have occurred after nightfall.

Suspicion fell on John Perry, who was hauled before the narrator, Sir Thomas Overbury, J.P. Perry stated that on the previous evening, about 8.45 p.m., he started for

Charringworth to seek his master, and explained to him that because he was afraid in the dark, he would go back and take Edward Harrison's horse and return. Perry followed through on his promise, and Reed dropped him off 'at Mr. Harrison's Court gate.' Perry lingered there till one Pierce passed by, and with Pierce (for reasons unknown), 'he went a bow's shot into the fields,' and thus returned to Harrison's gate. He now rested for an hour in a hen-coop, woke at midnight, and set off towards Charringworth again; the moon had now risen and alleviated his concerns. However, he got lost in the mist, slept along the roadside, and then went to Charringworth in the morning, only to discover that Harrison had been there the day before. Then he returned and met Edward Harrison, who was on his way to find his father at Charringworth.

Perry's account seems like an idiot delivered it, but Reed, Pierce, and two guys from Charringworth verified it to the best of their abilities. Perry had certainly been in company with Reed and Pierce the night before, say between nine and ten o'clock. If anything bad had happened to Harrison, it had to have happened before ten o'clock at night; if he were sober, he would not have stayed that late at Charringworth. Was he always sober? His wife and son's calm demeanor during his absence implies that he was a late-wandering old lad. They could have anticipated Perry to find him in his drinks and put him into bed in Charringworth or Ebrington.

Perry was kept in jail or, more oddly, in the inn until August 24. He narrated numerous stories, such as how a tinker or a servant killed his master and concealed him in a bean-rick, where a search revealed no est inventus. Harrison, along with the rents he had collected, faded into the blue. Perry now claimed that he would only tell Overbury everything. Perry said that Harrison was slain by his mother and brother, Joan and Richard Perry! His brother had looted the home the previous year with John Perry's guidance and connivance, while John 'had a Halibi,' being at church. According to John, the money was buried in the garden by the brother. It was sought but not discovered. He said that his tale about the 'two guys in white' who had earlier assaulted him in the yard was fiction. I might emphasize that that was not a rational man's lie. Perry was insane.

He continued with his tales. His mother and brother, he said, had often requested that he informed them when his employer went to collect rent. He'd done so after Harrison set off for Charringworth on August 16th. Next, John Perry described his trip with his brother on the evening of the fateful day. This statement contradicted both his prior narrative of his actions and the legitimate testimony of Reed and Pierce. Their truthful version crushed Perry's latest lie. Next, he said that he and Richard Perry had followed Harrison into Lady Campden's grounds when he returned home at night; Harrison had used a key to the private gate. Richard followed him into the grounds; after a little walk, John Perry joined him there and discovered his mother (how did she get there?) and Richard standing over the prone Harrison, whom Richard incontinently murdered. They took Harrison's money and planned to bury him "in the vast sink at Wallington's Mill." John Perry had abandoned them and had no idea if the corpse had been put into the sink. In truth, neither the sink nor the bean-rick was invented. John then described his encounter with Pierce but completely forgot about his meeting with Reed and failed to account for that aspect of his initial tale, which Reed and Pierce had both supported. The hat, comb, and band that John said he had transported away from Harrison's corpse, cut with his knife and tossed into the roadway. He didn't disclose where the blood on the band originated from.

Joan and Richard Perry were arrested and hauled before Overbury based on this incomprehensible jumble of mad lies. The sink and the Campden fish-pools and the wrecked remains of the house were searched in vain for Harrison's remains. On August 25, Overbury interrogated the three Perrys, and Richard and the mother denied everything John charged them with. John persisted with his account, and Richard confirmed that he and John had talked on the morning of Harrison's disappearance, 'but nothing passed between them to that purpose.'

A tragic event occurred as the three were being transported from Overbury's residence to Campden. Richard, who was a long-distance behind John, slipped 'a ball of inkle from his pocket.' When one of his guards took it up, Richard explained that it was "only his wife's hair-lace." However, there was a slip-knot at one end. The finder handed it to John, who had not seen his brother drop it since he was so far ahead. When shown the thread, John shook his head and remarked, "To his sorrow, he recognized it, for it was the cord his brother strangled his master with." At the next trial, John swore in response to this event.

In September, the Assizes were conducted, and the Perrys were indicted for both the robbery in 1659 and the murder in 1660. They pled 'Guilty' to the first accusation, as someone in court advised them to do since the offense was covered by Charles II's Act of Pardon and Oblivion, which was enacted during his positive Restoration. If they were innocent of the robbery, as they most likely were, they made a mistake by pleading guilty. We hear of no proof against them for the heist, except John's confession, which was maybe evidence against John but not against them. They harmed their case since, if they were indeed responsible for the heist at Harrison's residence, they were the most probable individuals in the neighborhood to rob him again and kill him. They most likely used the excellent King's indemnification to tie the rope around their necks. They eventually recanted their testimony and were most likely innocent of the crime in 1659.

They were not tried in September on the murder accusation. Sir Christopher Turner refused to continue 'because Harrison's corpse had not been recovered.' There was no corpus delicti, no proof that Harrison had died. Meanwhile, John Perry said, as if to underscore his insanity, that his mother and brother had attempted to poison him in jail! Sir B. Hyde, who was less legal than Sir Christopher

Turner, tried the Perrys for murder at the Spring Assizes in 1661. How he could accomplish this is unclear since the narrative of the trial is not in the Record House, and I am unable to locate it at the moment. John Wesley published a narrative in the Arminian Magazine about a man executed for killing another man, whom he later encountered in one of South America's Spanish colonies. I won't interrupt the Perrys' story to explain how a hung guy met a murdered man. Still, the incident demonstrates that inflicting death punishment for murder without evidence of murder is unconstitutional and injudicious. It was probably expected that Harrison, if alive, would have shown indications of life within nine or ten months.

All three Perrys pleaded 'not guilty at the spring trial' with John's confession being used against him. 'He told them he was then angry and knew not what he said,' he claimed. So there has to be some proof against Richard. He said that his brother had implicated others in addition to himself. When pressed to provide proof, he said that "most of those who had testified against him knew it," but he did not identify any of them. So evidence had been presented (perhaps to the effect that Richard was loaded with cash), but we don't know who gave it or what effect.

The Perrys were most likely not well-known. Joan, the mother, was said to be a witch. This allegation was seldom leveled against well-to-do persons. The legends and records of trials in Glanvil's Sadducismus Triumphatus reveal how great the dread of witches was at the time. Joan Perry, as a witch, was likely to be 'nane the waur o' a hanging,' according to her neighbors. She was executed first, with the notion that her death would eliminate any hypnotic or other evil effects she had on her boys, preventing them from confessing. We are unaware that the suggester's death removes post-hypnotic suggestion; the experiment has not been conducted. Joan's experiment was a failure. Poor Richard, who was executed next, could not persuade the 'dogged and sullen' John to clear his name with a deathbed statement. Such utterances were formerly believed to be irrefutable proof, at least in Scotland, except where it did not suit the Presbyterians to believe the dying man (as in George Sprot, killed for the Gowrie plot). When John was cut off, he remarked, 'he knew nothing of his master's death, nor what had become of him, but they may afterward (perhaps) hear.' Was John privy to something? It wouldn't surprise me if he were aware of the true situation of the case.

They did hear, but what they heard, and what I'm about to tell you, was completely unbelievable. Will Harrison, Gent., like the three stupid ewes in the folk-rhyme, 'come hirpling hame' after some years (presumably two). What had happened to the older adult? In a letter to Sir Thomas Overbury, he explained in a letter, but his story is as implausible as John Perry's.

He claims to have left his home in the afternoon (rather than the morning) on Thursday, August 16, 1660. He went to

Charringworth to collect rents, but all of Lady Campden's tenants were harvesting. When you think about it, August seems like an unusual month for rent collection. They arrived home late, which caused Harrison to be late till the end of the evening. He only got 23 l., which John Perry said was paid by one Edward Plaisterer during his first examination in 1660, and Plasterer confirmed. Harrison then traveled home, most likely in the darkness, and towards Ebrington, where the road was narrow and surrounded with whins, 'there met me one horseman who asked "Art thou there?"' Afraid of being ridden over, Harrison punched the horse on the nose, and the rider struck at him and stabbed him in the side with a sword. (The cut hat and bloody band were discovered at this section of the road, where the whins grew, but a stab in the side would not make a neck-band bloody.) Two more riders arrived; one of them shot Harrison in the leg. They did not remove his 23 l., but instead put him behind one of them on horseback, shackled him, and draped a large robe over him.

Is it plausible that highwaymen would have handcuffs that closed with a spring and a snap, as Harrison suggests? The narrative is entirely fiction, and it's a lousy one at that. Suppose abduction, rather than robbery, was the motivation (which would explain the handcuffs). What could any mortal stand gain by kidnapping, for the intention of selling him into slavery, a 'gent.' of seventy years of age?

They grabbed Harrison's money and 'tumbled me into a stone pit in the middle of the night. After an hour, they hauled him out again, and he understandably inquired what they wanted with him, given that they already had his money. One of these thugs shot Harrison again and placed a large amount of money into his pockets. What did they want with 23 l. if they had a lot of money? We hear of no other robberies in the area from which the money may have been obtained. And why does Harrison have to carry the money? (It has been proposed that to gain public favor, they pretended to be smugglers, and Harrison, with the money, pretended to be their valiant purser, wounded in some heroic adventure.)

They traveled till late on August 17, when they dropped Harrison off at a lonely cottage, bleeding and sorely bruised with the transport of the money.' They served their victim broth and brandy here. They rode all day Saturday to a home where they stayed and then carried Harrison to Deal and placed him down on Sunday. It was about three o'clock in the afternoon. If they had wished to get to the sea, they would have naturally gone to the west shore. While one guy was watching Harrison, two others met a guy, and 'I overheard them say seven pounds.' As Harrison later learned, the guy who suggested seven pounds (Crenshaw later learned— where?) indicated he felt Harrison would die before being placed on a ship. What diable was he going to do in this galère? On the other hand, Harrison was sent on board a casual vessel and stayed on board for six weeks.

What was the location of the land to which the ship would sail?

All the sailors know is how far ahead they are!

Harrison did not tell where the ship went roaming for six mortal weeks in the "foam of dangerous seas, amid faery realms lonely." Lord Bateman, for example:

He sailed eastward and westward.

Until he arrived in fabled Turkey.

Where he was apprehended and imprisoned

He was wear—ee! for the rest of his life!

'Then the Master of the ship arrived and informed me, and the other who was in the same predicament, that he detected three Turkish ships.' We're told that a full load of Harrisons was stolen and imprisoned aboard a ship released into the sea in the hopes that the captain would run across three Turkish rovers who would abduct them. At this pace, there must have been unexplained disappearances like Harrison's from dozens of English parishes in August 1660. If a crew of kidnappers had been capturing prisoners for personal fiscal reasons, they would have taken them to Virginian plantations, where Turkish galleys did not travel, and they would not have taken males over the age of seventy. Furthermore, kidnappers would not harm their hostages by stabbing them in the side and thigh if there was no resistance, as was done to Harrison.

'The remainder in the same condition' were 'dumped down' near Smyrna, where the precious Harrison was sold to a 'grave physician.'

This Turk was 87 years old and 'loved Crowland in Lincolnshire above all other areas in England.' Unfortunately, there are no recorded inquiries about a Turkish medical professional who previously practiced in Crowland, Lincolnshire, yet if he did, he was likely to be remembered in the area. Harrison used this Turk in the still room and as a laborer in the cotton fields, where he once knocked his slave down with his fist—pretty good for an eighty-seven-year-old Turk! He also gave Harrison (who worked in his company's chemical department) a "silver bowl, double gilt, to drink in, and dubbed him Boll"—his way of pronouncing bowl—no likely because he had acquired a Lincolnshire accent.

This Turk became sick on a Thursday and died the next Saturday when Harrison tramped to the closest port, bowl and all. Two sailors on a Hamburg ship denied him passage, but a third agreed to allow him on board for the price of his silver-gilt bowl. Harrison arrived in Lisbon without even his bowl when he met a guy from Wisbech, Lincolnshire. This kind Samaritan provided Harrison wine, strong waters, eight stivers, and transportation to Dover, from where he returned to Campden, much to the surprise of everyone. We don't know the identities of the ship or the captain that transported Harrison from Lisbon to Dover. The only person referenced in this dizzying tangle of insanity is Crenshaw (the guy seven pounds 'were mentioned').

'Many dispute the reality of this description Mr. Harrison

tells of himself, and his deportation, thinking he was never out of England,' writes the editor of our booklet. I'm not surprised by their skepticism. We are informed that Harrison had 'all his days been a man of sober life and discourse' and that he 'left behind him a significant amount of his Lady's money in his home.' On the night of his disappearance, he did not see any of the Perrys. The editor concedes that Harrison, as a commodity, was not worth the freight to Deal, much alone Smyrna. His son took over as Lady Campden's steward in his absence, and he acted horribly in that role. Some assumed that this son planned Harrison's capture, but if so, why did he secure John Perry's hanging, in chains, on Broadway hill, 'where he may daily view him'?

That might be a blind spot. But Harrison could not have expected John Perry to help him by implicating himself, his brother, and his mother, which was the most unexpected thing in the world. He had no idea that his father would return from Charringworth in the dark on August 16, 1660, and arrange for three riders armed with a great weight of money to stab and take off the aging patriarch. Young Harrison had not a big fardel of money to offer them, and since they were already so wealthy, what did they stand to gain by transporting Harrison to Deal and placing him on board a casual ship with "others in the same condition"? They might have left him in the stone-pit:' he had no idea who they were, and the longer they rode by daylight, with a hatless, shackled, and severely injured prisoner, his pockets bulging with money, the greater the chance of being discovered. So a group of three guys cycles across England in broad daylight, from Gloucestershire to Deal. Behind one of them lies a wounded, hatless, shackled victim with overflowing pockets. Nobody suspects anything, and no one alerts a judge to this great maneuver! It's much too ludicrous!

Harrison's narrative is obviously and childishly untrue. These strange horsemen must have been confronted at every baiting spot and inn. If Harrison were telling the truth, he would have identified the ship and captain that carried him to Dover.

After dismissing Harrison's tale, we wonder what may have caused his absence. On the evening of August 16, he strolled to within half a mile of his residence. He would not have done so if he had been intent on a senile amour involving his disappearance from home, and if that were his intention, he would have equipped himself with money. Again, a fit of 'ambulatory somnambulism,' with the formation of a split or dual personality and forgetting his true name and address, seems unlikely to have struck him at that precise time and location. If it occurred, he couldn't hurry out in a mob and travel discreetly across the countryside since there were no trains.

Again, the notion of ambulatory somnambulism fails to explain his chopped hat and bloodied band, which were discovered near the whins on the road beyond Ebrington. His narrative does not account for them either. He claims he was stabbed in the side and thigh. This would not result in the amputation of his headgear or the exsanguination of his band. On the other hand, he would leave pools and traces of blood on the road, dubbed "the highway." But there was nothing further discovered,' no pools or evidence of blood on the road. As a result, the cut hat and bloodied band were a deliberate false trail, not put there by John Perry, as he falsely claimed, but by someone else.

The implication is that Harrison's presence in Campden was inconvenient for someone. He had gone through the most trying moments and had found himself in a new situation with new rulers. He knew something about the turbulent times: he was a witness who should be kept out of the way. He may have kept a secret about one of the Regicides' cases or private interests since he was a loyal servant of a wealthy family. As a result, he was carried away, leaving an almost probably false trail—the cut hat and bleeding band. By a strange coincidence, his servant, John Perry, became insane—he was not rational on Thursday, August 16, and implicated himself, his brother, and his mother. During the two or three years that Harrison was missing, he was most likely never far from Campden. It was certainly made worthwhile for him to return and recount his crazy narrative, as well as accept the circumstance. There is no alternative explanation that 'collides the facts.' ' We'll never know what Harrison knew or why his absence was so important. But he was never a prisoner in 'famous Turkee.' 'It is hard to give a sufficient incentive for kidnapping the elderly man... considerable profit was not expected to result from the selling of the elderly man as a slave,' says Mr Paget. There was no profit, particularly given that the elderly guy was delivered in a damaged and damaged state. But finding a reason to keep Harrison out of the way is difficult since we don't know anything about his neighbours' private lives. Roundheads among them may have had compelling motives to keep Harrison imprisoned until the Restoration's vengeance were exacted. According to this perspective, the enigma virtually ceases to be strange since such insane self-accusations as John Perry's are not unusual.

www.ingramcontent.com/pod-product-compliance
Lightning Source LLC
Chambersburg PA
CBHW061041050726

47592CB00004B/1535